THE IR COMMUNICATION HANDBOOK

A CHECKLIST

Jonathan L. Passmore

ISBN: 978-0-578-18035-9 (sc)
ISBN: 978-0-578-18131-8 (e)

Valor IR Consulting LLC
45 Sherman St, Fairfield, CT, USA
203-258-2880
Valor IR Consulting LLC

Lulu Publishing Services rev. date: 8/17/2016

To my friends and colleagues in the investment markets
of the world whose behaviors, wisdom, personalities and
passion have all contributed to the creation of this book.

and

To the Investor Relations professional determined
to stay ahead in the digital world

CONTENTS

ACKNOWLEDGEMENTS

David Bowers, friend and co-founder of Absolute Strategy Research for suggesting and inspiring this idea in the first place;

Kristina Zucchi, friend, former colleague and journalist for her help in editing and correcting my manuscript and translating my English into American;

Marissa Beringer, also friend and former colleague for helping me navigate my way through technology, often to little avail.

INTRODUCTION

So why write this book, and why now?

I joined the market back in 1975, in the City of London more than a decade before Big Bang somewhat civilized that marketplace, introducing a more structured, egalitarian and performance-based culture to the storied Square Mile.

Communications were unsophisticated in the 70's, to put it mildly: young trainee brokers (like me) being yelled at unmercifully by incoherent, well-dressed thugs (that was before lunch – they seldom worked beyond 11:30 am); telex machine bells tinkling musically around the fringes of the trading floor, bringing messages from the other side of the world at the speed of a turtle; large boxes of white chalk used for market pricing on blackboards, in exotica such as Eurodollar CD's, Bankers' Acceptances and the like.

In the 1980's, now resident in New York, I marveled at the development of the Telerate system, recognizing that my clients, by looking at the screens I installed in their offices, now had access to all the market intelligence I had previously provided. A loss of influence? The first signs of bigger changes to come?

Well, yes. Progress accelerated over the next 20 years through the adoption of information services such as Bloomberg and Reuters, the development of in-house information and trading systems, the growth of the Internet and the evolution of social media and its broadening impact and influence over an increasingly widespread and knowledgeable audience.

So in a world adopting digital solutions at break-neck speed, why would I focus on that most analog of activities, personal communication?

Because it matters!

Millenials can be forgiven for thinking that the world revolves around their gadgets – information, communication and the Kardashians with a swipe of a touchscreen. But should they be forgiven for forgetting that all of these "connections" are but our servants, designed to educate, connect and entertain us in our daily lives? When technology becomes an end in itself, rather than the means to an end, we lose something and that is what this book will attempt to both illustrate and delay.

What remains critical to the people on this planet (in truth, this book is not just about IR, it has broader social and business ramifications) is the ability to connect, one to another, whether in business, in education, in love; the list is endless.

And connection takes skill, even more so in an era of texts and other social media where the facial expression that enhances or blunts the message is lost; where the inflection of the voice that defines the message's true meaning is unheard; and where the body language of a liar remains undetected.

This book will attempt to convince you that maintaining personal interconnection is essential. And most importantly it will provide a repeatable methodology to guide you to efficient, relevant and timely communications.

We'll take a walk through the thickets of meeting preparation in a systematic, organized way. But in order to get prepared, you need to understand the expectations that all parties could and should have, the influence that the IR professional can bring to bear, and the pitfalls that can trap the unwary (i.e. the unprepared).

The purpose of this book is to help you be on top of your game; get organized to satisfy your investors; burnish your company's reputation; and best of all, make you look good (especially with your senior management).

If you can raise your game in the IR communications world, you may achieve the holy grail of stock performance: strength when times are good, and resilience when times are tough.

As a Portfolio Manager for many years who was the primary communicator with our plan sponsor clients, I found it consistently true that outperformance in a down market was always better received than strong performance in an up market. And what makes stocks outperform, especially when the environment is poor?

First class communication.

So let's get started.

CHAPTER ONE

THE EXPECTATIONS PRINCIPLE

*"There is only one thing about which I am certain, and that
is that there is very little about which one can be certain."*
W. Somerset Maughan

Expectations dominate our lives. We live by them, we try to live up to them. We impose them upon ourselves and on others. They range from the mild or inconsequential ("the forecast should be fine; let's have a BBQ" – me, last summer), to the historic ("England expects every man to do his duty" – Admiral Horatio Nelson, Battle of Trafalgar, 1805); from the literary ("Great Expectations" – Charles Dickens, 1860) to the parental ("I expect you to be tucked up in bed, homework done, by the time I get back!" – some of you, last night).

Plenty of opportunities, for success and failure.

Opportunities for participants to excel or underperform; to be excited or disappointed. Expectations and their fulfillment (or lack thereof) represent an equation that is present in almost every part of our lives: in relationships, business, politics, entertainment and, of course, investing.

A successful IR officer needs to have investor expectations in mind when he or she thinks about what and how to communicate to shareholders.

What are those expectations?

An investor wants to participate in useful, relevant meetings that will contribute to a growing familiarity with your company. And when an investor sees and hears a well-run, transparent company communicating effectively, the expectations of a strong and resilient stock will naturally grow.

But surely stock prices are affected by much more than just communications! What about external factors over which there is no control? Like economics, for example? It is true that doing business in a market where GDP is shrinking or inflation is high is a poor recipe for growing sales and expanding margins, regardless of what the investor relations officer says.

How about internal performance? If the company's sales and margins are growing and its ingenuity and enterprise as expressed by new products and services is accelerating, the IRO's commentary to already satisfied investors is merely icing on a well baked, tasty cake.

But consider this. The greatest influence on a company's stock is not its performance in absolute terms, but its performance AGAINST EXPECTATIONS. And who supplies those expectations? The company itself through that conduit of all things relevant and germane, the investor relations officer.

Before we go deeper into expectations, why do we think a strong stock price is important anyway? This might seem pretty obvious but think of the constituents who are affected by gyrations in market value:

Shareholders – the providers of capital who need to be kept satisfied lest you come asking for more;

Executives – whose pay is increasingly tied to company performance and distributed in stock;

Employees – beyond those with ESOPs, a sturdy stock price, the most public and readily available indication of a company's health can boost morale, discourage staff turnover and ignite ambition;

IR officers – answerable, at some level, to all of the above, you will bask in their affections when the going is good and merit grudging praise if your efforts in poor environments create the resilience craved by all.

The best companies, like all good communicators, manage expectations expertly. With customers they create anticipation for new products and services; with employees, potential for better pay and promotional opportunities; with shareholders, strong performance in a mix of market conditions plus the promise of dividends and share buybacks.

As the creator of expectations, the company controls the conversation, essential if the narrative is important to you. Of course, with that control comes enhanced risk. If you fail to meet the expectations you have so carefully crafted, the reaction will be more severe than if you had said nothing at all. Do you have a choice? In a world where communications and access to information are so widespread, silence is a very poor option.

Expectations cannot always be managed to your satisfaction. They will always fall victim to the unexpected, notably in the case of a change in the economic cycle or an unexpected trauma at the company. Well thought out assumptions made by management and investors alike can easily become irrelevant when the environment changes unexpectedly.

A word about guidance.

Investors use several inputs to develop an opinion about a stock's future potential: their internally-generated, fundamental research; sell-side recommendations and consensus; and the Company's own guidance. Corporate guidance is a formal assessment of future potential including an assumption about market conditions and the ability of the company to perform during the economic cycle. Any interruption or distortion of those assumptions and assessments will have an impact on expectations.

IR officers should always remember that the extent to which the company matches, lags or outperforms the market is of great concern to shareholders. The degree to which it matters depends entirely on how well performance meets the <u>expectations</u> held by the shareholders. And that depends on the IR team and the quality of their communication.

As economies and markets respond to external stimuli and move through their cycles, so will the positions at the fund manager. In times of crisis and market weakness, fund managers will hedge or sell their positions. In times of growth and recovery, managers will use cash or leverage the portfolio to add to their most promising positions.

Deciding which holdings are sold or bought depends, to a large degree, on how much the manager knows and understands each company. And the quality of that knowledge will depend, to an equally large degree on the relationship established and the trust developed between the IR Officer and the shareholder.

In simple terms, if a market has peaked and is moving into a period of weakness, the fund manager has a choice: top slice all of the holdings in the fund thereby reducing overall exposure, or select certain stocks for a trim or outright elimination to achieve the same goal. IR officers should understand that managers are generally reluctant to make wholesale changes to their portfolios. It is expensive and may not suit the style of the portfolio. If a manager has confidence that a stock in the portfolio will exhibit resilience in a downturn and outperform the market, a trim may be minor or not occur at all. And that will arise from sound, clear, concise communication that is useful and relevant to the listener.

So, expectations are a function of communications.

And each communication is a point of influence for the IR Officer.

CHAPTER TWO

IT TAKES TWO TO TANGO

*"It takes two to speak the truth – one
to speak and another to hear."*
Henry David Thoreau

So far, you're on the hook! You create expectations and manage the variability of those expectations between the demands of your executives and your investors, all the while adopting a demeanor that is open, erudite, wise, compliant (in a legal sense) and professional.

But don't forget, it takes two to tango. There is yin and yang in much of life, including investing. Presenter and listener; question and answer; expectations and fulfillment. All of these combinations are points of influence for the IR professional.

As stated earlier, investors have expectations: a greater understanding of the company's business; comprehensive answers to fundamental questions; knowledge of the market, its challenges and opportunities; with the objective of creating a personal connection and thereby establishing trust. Put another way, the investor's fulfillment will come from relevant communications from well-prepared executives who understand the investor's needs and <u>also</u> want to build a relationship.

It is hard to overstate the importance of communications with investors.

Put yourself in their shoes for a moment and recognize the challenge of the role – committing large sums of money to investments based on an assessment of imperfectly known and understood variables that will only prove to be truly right or wrong in retrospect. (The finest "investors" invariably prove to be those with 20-20 hindsight and includes many that don't have to pull the trigger!)

In addition, the investor is afflicted by the variability of expectations. Just because company guidance has been published, for example, doesn't ensure that every investor will interpret that information in the same way. As a result, the response of the market may not be what the company or the investor expected.

Each investor understands that the very nature of investing requires imprecision. If we had perfect knowledge about every company and the environment in which they operated, investing would be perfectly predictable and very, very boring. Fair disclosure regulations and pre-release "quiet" periods dictate that investors spend an enormous amount of time and effort anticipating the consequences of their expectations. So anything that can add an element of precision to this imprecise world is valuable.

The Yin:

Which brings us back to you, the IR officer, and the communication of what is legal and proper under Stock Exchange regulations. In short, companies should make the most of the latitude they are given under the law, communicating to the fullest extent allowable. Anything less is a wasted opportunity for which there is no excuse.

And that means tackling the tough issues as well as the successes, especially around results.

Most of the time, investors would rather gain insight into the potential problems at a company – weak operations; a pending law suit; loss of a patent. Concerns can fester if not dealt with promptly, clearly and completely.

If a weakness in sales, earnings or margins is left unexplained, investors will fear the worst and take remedial action. And if that developing pessimism leads to a sell, the investor will seldom reverse that decision and reestablish a position in the short-term. Too many unanswered questions and unanticipated movements in the stock price lead the investor to fear he lacks a comprehensive understanding of the company, and creates a powerful motive for future avoidance. Once bitten, twice shy, etc.

Advice: Prompt, clear, complete communications may not always prevent an investor from dismounting from a stock, but a full explanation today, even if its bad news, can create enough credibility to warrant revisiting the stock at a later date. Overall, an investor will be less unhappy about losses on a stock he realizes has changed, than on one he never really understood in the first place.

So master the bad details as well as the good. Understand the investor will want answers to what's wrong, more than what's right, and prepare accordingly. Good news is easy to deliver: how you handle the communication of harsh realities will determine your place in the investor's mind, and the portfolio.

And remember that no-one understands the ebbs and flows of the cycle better than investors. Apart from a handful of star managers, the majority of the best fund managers outperform often, but not all of the time. When they underperform, their clients will often refrain from hitting the sell button, AS LONG AS THEY FULLY UNDERSTAND WHY THE UNDERPERFORMANCE IS TAKING PLACE AND WHAT THE ASSET MANAGER IS DOING ABOUT IT.

The Yang:

Once you've embarked on that strategy, the strategy of total disclosure, embracing the problems as fiercely as the successes, you're entitled to your own expectations of how you want the relationship to develop. At the very least you'll want an investor who will trust you enough to maintain his or her holding when the company is firing on 6 or 7 cylinders rather than 8.

Just as asset managers can underperform, companies will succeed some but not all of the time. External forces or internal issues may cause a disruption in performance from time to time. If you spend as much time (or maybe more) explaining why your revenues and margins have slipped or your new product launch has been soft, your investors will give you the benefit of the doubt. But be warned: keep silent and suffer the consequences.

So having spent time planning how to deal with the tough stuff (and as a result, gain the respect of the investor) you will find it much easier to express what's important to you and your company. If the investor's short-term concerns are addressed, he will be much more willing to listen to your ideas of long-term business development, variations in guidance, and management succession updates that will elevate you from parrot of quarterly results to a serious investment partner worthy of a longer-term commitment.

In essence, what you're trying to do is differentiate yourself from the competition. Not just your corporate nemesis who makes a similar product or offers a cheaper service, but from every other investment option that your investor may be considering at any given time.

Advice: Be proactive. In certain circumstances like earnings announcements, you may be constrained from pre-emptive behavior, but regular contact with your largest investors about relevant market information, for example, can go a long way to developing the relationship both are seeking. In the event that an unexpected issue hits the headlines, reaching out to investors with comments before they call you is a sure-fire way of raising credibility. Don't feel a complete explanation is necessary in those early hours after an announcement. It is preferable, of course, but the knowledge that a company is 1) working the problem, and 2) is contacting major shareholders to keep them appraised of the process will help forestall any knee-jerk selling that inevitably results from a state of ignorance.

Expectations for both investors and corporate executives are closely intertwined through the common objective of a successful stock.

And fulfillment for both parties will come from first-class communications with investors who will be left with better understanding, greater knowledge and growing trust, REGARDLESS OF RECENT PERFORMANCE.

CHAPTER THREE

THE ART OF COMMUNICATION

"Is sloppiness in speech caused by ignorance or apathy? I don't know and I don't care."
William Safire

The act of communication is something we take for granted. We are taught to talk as toddlers. Our first attempts at writing soon follow. But before too long, the act of conversing or putting pen to paper (or tapping out a message on a keyboard) becomes second nature.

As we get older, the actual ART of communication becomes more or less important depending on the route our lives follow. To the student in the debating society looking for a career in law, politics or sales, verbal skills are of paramount importance. For the budding author or analyst, the ability to write clearly, succinctly and in an entertaining fashion is key.

And then there are those for whom communicating is relegated to the far back burner, their expectations of needing to talk or write for a living so low as to make their vocal chords and hand-writing skills almost redundant. Except for asking directions and writing thank you notes, of course.

But for people in the investment business, and especially among the investor relations ranks, communication is the mother's milk, a core competency, a skill without which the job becomes immeasurably harder.

IRO's are expected to be eloquent speakers and fluent writers, capable of articulating complex concepts in ways that do not frustrate the specialist but can inform the generalist. The goal is to educate the audience, provide facts where available and reasoned guidance where appropriate. The delivery must avoid verbosity but provide enough detail and substance to be of value, anticipating what is required and bypassing the inconsequential.

Confidence must be projected in your delivery but complacency and hubris that will damage credibility must be avoided.

And all the while IROs must be listeners too. Because the posing of a question by a member of the audience, especially in one-on-one meetings demonstrates beyond all doubt that you have achieved the major goal of ENGAGEMENT!

For the investor, listening to a presentation and being unable to ask a clarifying question of a speaker entranced by his or her own eloquence is like asking a starving man to say Grace. By paying close attention to the body language of the investor, by noticing the sudden change in posture, the _eagerness_ to ask a question, you pay the listener the compliment of inviting them to being part of a dialogue, not the victim of a monologue.

Depending on which social scientist you prefer, 90-95% of communication is non-verbal. So recognizing body language is another skill you need to develop along with developing a positive body language of your own. Just as you should be aware of your audience, your ability to project confidence, maintain eye contact and calmly respond to difficult questions without defensive gestures, will all add to the positive image you want to portray. Your words are key but your body language has the potential to add or detract from your essential message.

Advice: To imagine yourself in a meeting environment is to practice the art of communication.

Imagine what you want to project: confidence, competence, fluency, empathy and humility. And while that is a lot to pack into a one-hour meeting, including these components will reap its reward!

- *Confidence* at the start of a meeting settles the participants into the right frame of mind so the meeting will not be wasted;
- *Competence* is essential but going beyond basic expectations of the occasion is a welcome plus;
- *Fluency* promotes credibility and confirms your right to be there;
- *Empathy* proves you know your investor and the experience they have had with your stock;
- And *humility*, whether your stock is lagging or lapping the benchmark, will display your understanding that every investor's story is unique.

Great communicators cultivate their art for several purposes: to inform, amuse, enlighten, delight, prepare, warn and scold, to name but a few. But above all there is the desire, the need to influence.

Winston Churchill used his wartime speeches to comfort, strengthen and prepare the British public during the country's darkest days in World War Two. With the power of his words he influenced his listeners into doubling down on hardship, going the extra mile in effort and suffering through bombing, rationing and personal loss. While even the worst performance of a company's stock should never be compared to the Blitz, on occasion you will need to produce a narrative that persuades your investor to look beyond current discomfort and be confident that sufficient potential lies ahead to make that discomfort worthwhile.

The presentation that you make to your investor is an opportunity to influence their thinking, to mold an opinion that aligns with everyone's expectations. You cannot achieve that by sheer force of personality (although some have tried) nor by falsifying the facts (ditto) but the manner of your delivery and the clarity of your explanation can combine to give investors the confidence they need.

The ability to influence others is developed by the adoption of a reasonable tone telling a plausible story that has an acceptable outcome. When told with integrity, bad news can be delivered with a higher chance of acceptance. Bad news is never welcomed but when delivered appropriately can be absorbed and accepted without hysteria, accusations or pain.

So having decided on the "human" tone you want to adopt, you can start to prepare for THE MEETING!

CHAPTER FOUR

MEETING PREPARATION (1)

*"The prime purpose of eloquence is to
keep other people from talking"*
Louis Vermeil

Your expectations are set, you know what you want to achieve. You have divined your purpose and decided on a message you want (or need) to deliver. Now you must establish **what** you want to say, to **whom, how** (in what medium) and **when**. It is time to get down to the serious business of meeting preparation, without which your time, effort and money will surely be wasted. With preparation your meetings will run smoothly and your audience will be satisfied, at least by the organization of the meeting if not the message! As I have mentioned, bad news is always more palatable when delivered clearly and professionally: you should <u>never</u> give investors an additional reason for selling a stock beyond their assessment of the business case.

You need knowledge to deliver knowledge effectively.

Simply put, the company's representative must:

- recognize common problems;
- know his or her subject;
- know the audience;

- be part of a coherent, well-prepared team;
- avoid obvious mistakes.

Diligent preparation will achieve these objectives while accepting that the unexpected question is always lurking there with the ability to surprise. But confidence in one's material and presentation skills provides an excellent foundation for dealing with surprises off-the-cuff; comprehensive preparation that includes anticipation of such tangential topics helps minimize that risk.

The most common problems in meetings include the following:

- not knowing (or understanding) your audience;
- delivering a message that is incomplete or confusing;
- using a standardized pitch that covers every possible permutation of investor concerns but lacks focus;
- ignorance of market concerns, about recent results or trends within the company;
- lack of connection to the big picture (sector or economy);
- lack of awareness about competitive threats.

The idea that you should know your subject might seem a little obvious: you don't send a banking analyst to talk about yoghurt! But being well-versed in your topic allows you to calibrate the message to your audience. Detailed presentations about biological reactions at the molecular level are as confusing to the generalist as discussing product labelling would be meaningless to the specialist. By having the skill to go broad and deep, you can adapt to every audience.

Knowing your audience is the best way to connect to your investor. Working towards a knowledgeable, trusting relationship is the core purpose of this book. If you are ignorant of what drives your audience, how can you tailor a meeting to satisfy their needs? Maximizing a 60-minute meeting would be nigh impossible between perfect strangers.

What do you need to know about your investor?

- How big are they, in terms of assets under management and people?
- What is their investment style? Depending on whether they are long-only; long-short; activist; growth; value; GARP; fundamental; technical; passive; active, you can arguably adapt your presentation to appeal to their style;
- Who are you meeting with – the Portfolio Manager or an Analyst? If the PM, is he or she a generalist, a sector specialist, running Global money or a single-country fund? If an Analyst, how experienced are they? If both a generalist PM and sector Analyst are attending, be prepared to appeal to both.
- Is this a first-time meeting requiring a different level of detail?
- What has the investor's experience been with your stock? When did they buy it and has it been a good experience for them?
- How much do they own (relative to your market cap and their AUM)?
- Who participated in previous meetings and what topics were discussed? Do you have notes that can establish a continuity between meetings? The investor probably does!

Having a sense of the mood of the investor going into the meeting can be very helpful. If their experience with your stock has been problematic, they may be waiting for an excuse to dump you. A bad, poorly prepared meeting will surely qualify! Being empathetic with your shareholder may not save the day if they are determined to exit your stock but at least their decision will be made on fundamentals and not because you fumbled and stumbled your way through the meeting.

Having context between the current discussion and previous meetings enhances the dialogue and reassures the investor that not only are you willing to share meaningful information but that you have thought about their earlier concerns. This is particularly relevant in the follow-up to a bad meeting: (the fact that you even have a chance of a follow-up justifies optimism). And bad meetings happen: to be able to re-address the controversy that sparked some animosity or concern demonstrates your willingness to deal with the tough stuff, helping to clear the air.

Of course, a key part of the meeting preparation is selecting the right company representatives. Investor Relations Officers, by virtue of their constant contact with the investment community are an obvious first choice for a standard presentation, especially if they are empowered to speak comprehensively on behalf of their employer.

But many investors ask to speak to CEO's and CFO's, not just to hear information (which should be identical to that imparted by their IRO's!) but to have a glimpse of the vision and skill of the management team that is guiding their investment.

Advice: This is where coaching becomes a key component of meeting preparation; while senior executives are (and should be) well-versed in all aspects of their company's activities, they may shy away from awkward questions that directly challenge their stewardship of the firm. They <u>have</u> to answer those questions: a failure to do so will cause lasting damage to the company's reputation.

Of course, the opposite is also true: the chief executive who takes the hard questions head on and answers them in detail, builds the brand and strengthens the relationship considerably.

So once the meeting team is selected, the final task is to identify the roles of each attendee. Just as a meeting with a sole representative who can't answer any questions is a waste of everyone's time, so is a meeting attended by eight people of whom only two have a speaking role a waste of the host's coffee.

A corporate update provided by two or three senior representatives, all of whom have a defined role allows a number of possibilities: the investor can meet and question key executives; the representatives can tag-team the responses, ensuring that no key issues are left out; and the relationship opportunity is expanded beyond a single person or department at the company.

Basic mistakes are legion in the investment business despite the fact that the vast majority of executives who have public-facing roles behave in an exemplary fashion. However, we should always be on the lookout for errors of omission, commission and, of course, outright stupidity.

Three examples spring to mind:

- **Biting the hand that feeds you.** A large Russian company that launched an ADR program in the mid-1990's was an early favorite with hedge funds, the initial source of capital for many emerging market listings. After several years of popularity and market cap leadership, the CFO on a roadshow to the United States expressed disdain at having to meet with a large, influential hedge fund in Texas, preferring to hob-nob with large long-only managers (despite their lack of interest in Russia).
  Explanation: Hedge funds then, and now, have been a major influence on capital flows and comprise a small but powerful community who talk to each other – a lot. Disrespecting a major member of that community would have lasting consequences.

- **Misunderstanding what investors want to hear.** A major chemical company was asked if it planned to raise wages for its employees, a policy that was being adopted by hundreds of companies in its market and sector. Had the company demurred for financial reasons, it might have been acceptable but the reason given was that their "employees would only waste the money and it would be better not to tempt them".

Explanation: Adopting a feudal attitude toward employees does little to persuade an investor that labor relations will be peaceful in the future and raises the specter of a brain drain to competitors.

- **Preferring tea over coffee.** A widely-held consumer electronics company was losing share in new products and the CFO on a roadshow to the United States invited several members of a large pension fund investment team to a meeting in New York. Halfway through the meeting he fell fast asleep, and resisted the admittedly delicate attempts by his subordinates to wake him. After a while the investment team left and minutes later sold the stock.

  Explanation: Jet lag is a curse for many business travelers and meeting preparation should include rest as well as homework. Meeting schedules should be prepared with such mundane issues in mind.

Advice: Decide the purpose of the meeting; be up to date on your subject; know your audience; understand their mood; select your team and define their roles.

It is now time to create a pitch book that matches that purpose, but can also enhance your brand, inform your audience and become a relevant, professional reference resource for your company.

CHAPTER FIVE
MEETING PREPARATION (2)

*"I'm going to make a long speech because I've
not had the time to prepare a short one."*
Winston Churchill

How many investors have sat in their conference rooms, eager with anticipation for the meeting to start, only to feel their heart sink as the 100-page presentation deck hits the table with a resounding thud?

How many portfolio managers and analysts have leafed through the pitch book desperately seeking something that might add some clarity to an unfamiliar but tantalizing story?

How many shareholders have cast aside an impenetrable book, shakily confident that despite the confusing nature of the information contained therein, the IR Officer in front of them will explain all, lift the clouds of uncertainty around the corporate story, reveal the catalysts that will pull the company from the doldrums, spark renewed confidence in the story and justify the hopes of the audience?

A little hyperbolic you might say?

But in a world where competition for the institutional investor's attention is getting more and more intense, any advantage you can bring that educates and helps the investment professional in their decision-making capacity is of huge value! And that begins with the presentation book.

The book has several roles:

- To **support** the face-to-face presentation made by the company's representatives;
- To **act** as a reference for the investment team in their archives;
- To **fill in** the gaps that the company deems important but may not be addressed in the one-on-one meeting;
- To **provide** relevant, clear, concise information to people unable to attend a roadshow meeting.

That's a big responsibility for a book but one that can be achieved successfully with appropriate thought and preparation.

So what should be included in the perfect pitch book? You know your audience (assuming you read the earlier chapters!), have your own purpose and want to educate and inform the investor.

Given you probably don't want to create an individual book for each client, some suggestions for "must-haves" that will satisfy a broad audience include:

- **Brief corporate description** - useful for first time attendees even when they are joining more familiar colleagues;
- **Recent financials** – including a comparison versus expectations. Absolute numbers are valuable but the investor's reaction will be magnified by earlier expectations, so include your guidance;
- **Corporate excellence** - focus on the product/service/business unit that is driving your recent success. In the event of a miss, equal emphasis on what has not worked and where the solution lies;

- **Long-term guidance** - with changes. Trends are just as important as absolute numbers and your changing guidance will say a lot about your expectations;
- **Segments targeted for investment & growth** - essential for the long-term investor's understanding of your strategy;
- **Segments targeted for closure or sale** - evidence of a clear-eyed vision of the future;
- **Returns to shareholders** - the existence or lack of meaningful returns can trigger discussions on cash generation, capex, etc.;
- **Debt ratios and service costs** - more crucial as interest rates seem set to rise;
- **Hedging strategies** - if engaged in global trade/activities, your exposure to volatile currency moves warrants explanation;
- **SRI/ESG initiatives** - corporate governance and sustainability improvements/developments should be emphasized;

Advice: There may be other items pertinent to your story that need to be discussed. But remember, you have 45-60 minutes to make the points that you believe are essential to understanding your story – don't waste them.

Subjects to avoid, in the interests of time, efficiency and maintaining a good relationship:

- **Ancient history** - the origins of the company are not relevant to the present, unless the company is a recent start-up;
- **Deep dive financial data** - PM's will look to understand the impact of financials but a detailed analysis can be taken off-line;
- **Small/irrelevant segments** - unless they are due for investment or closure;
- **Complex flow charts** that are hard to read or explain.

The best definition of a successful deck is one that can be easily shared by someone who has only heard the story once.

Similar to the "elevator pitch" it describes a narrative that can be related in simple, clear, effective terms and fully understood. Anything less increases the burden on both the speaker and the listener to relate and comprehend the message. Presentation decks should be an integral part of the practice sessions the management team has undergone.

In these last two chapters there has been much emphasis on tailoring your remarks (and to a similar degree, your presentation) to the needs of the investor.

In the real world, conference calls and conference presentations have broadly diverse audiences and a fairly generic approach is the only reasonable option. But with one-on-one meetings, you get to see the whites of their eyes and a different approach is merited.

Of course, it often happens that road show schedules are completed at the last minute, leaving little time to do the all-important analysis of your audience. But for the majority of your meetings, the investor will be identified and thorough preparation is possible.

You may rely on your organizing broker or an external source for data about the size, methods, skills and experience of the asset manager you are about to meet. But in the absence of meaningful information, call the investor and find out what would make an effective, valuable meeting.

CHAPTER SIX

PROACTIVITY

*"Never put off until tomorrow what you can
put off until the day after tomorrow"*
Mark Twain

Management of expectations, communicated clearly and effectively, will resonate with the investment community and be reflected in the performance of your stock.

To summarize the earlier chapters (clearly and effectively!), the investor relations team has decided on a purpose for a communication with shareholders, prepared the team and developed the materials required to convey the message.

The conference call takes place, the non-deal roadshow is completed, the industry conference presentation is delivered and the media are informed. What now?

Sadly, for the over-worked, probably under-appreciated IR professional whose head has been spinning with all of the extra labor this book recommends, there will be no resting on laurels or basking in the glory of a job well done. Not yet, anyway.

Because along with the satisfaction of having organized a well-run distribution of relevant information to the investment community comes additional responsibility. Follow-up with investors; calls that need returning; post-hoc questions that require answers; compiling and filing of meeting notes; development of a new, proactive communication strategy – the job is never finished.

Following up on issues that were unresolved at a meeting is essential. It can be acceptable for an IR Officer (although not for a CEO or CFO) to admit ignorance on a specific topic and pledge to get back to the enquirer. Only occasionally, though! Too many "I don't know" responses will quickly undermine the credibility and value of your presence – not a situation you seek.

But in that event, a prompt, comprehensive response will quickly satisfy and resolve any disappointment felt by the investor, who can now complete his review, make his recommendation and move on to pastures new.

The completion of that follow-up request is part of what should become a comprehensive record of communications between your company and all of its major investors. Good note keeping might seem remarkably pedestrian in the 21st century but this is more than keeping accurate records. A long-term narrative of discussions between the two parties can be referenced in future meetings, both for context in looking at contemporary issues but also as a subtle reminder that you have the investor's detailed thoughts about your company close at hand.

In addition, good notes become useful for other members of your IR team including senior executives or Board members who may become engaged in the investor relations process at some future date.

Follow-up and notes are part of the historical content of your relationship. But the other responsibility you should develop with your core investors is that of proactive behavior.

This simply describes how the well-organized IR Officer can reach out to investors, between regularly scheduled announcements on matters of importance to the company.

COMPLIANCE CHECK: This is not in any way meant to breach Fair Disclosure regulations. This would not include information about earnings or sales or any hard facts that could allow one investor to have an information advantage over any other.

But back to proactive behaviors. The most straightforward example would be about industry announcements in the media that do not directly affect the company but about which it might be expected to have an opinion.

Another example could be where the company has made an announcement about its activities through the financial media and the IRO wants to make sure that key investors have seen the tape. The IRO could field specific questions about the announcement and reflect them back to senior management for a response.

But perhaps the most critical example might be during a corporate crisis where a response from the company is not only desired, but essential.

When corporate disasters occur, the response from the investment community can be swift and ruthless. Depending on the nature of the crisis, one can understand why an asset manager would shoot first and ask questions later. Markets are relentless and punish the indecisive.

But if you put yourself in the shoes of a Portfolio Manager or Analyst for a moment, it is not hard to understand why they push the sell button.

The most common triggers for a sell during a crisis are:

- A lack of information about developments;
- Denials by the company about the severity of the problem.

Early calls from the investor relations team might not answer or solve either of those issues, but they might give the Portfolio Manager a reason to pause.

Imagine these scenarios:

A large multinational experiences a major catastrophe at a critical production facility in the United States, in time for the evening news broadcast but well past the stock market close. Asset managers who own the stock see the bulletin which describes the problem but not what caused it. What do they do?

In one scenario, neither the PM nor the Analyst know whom to call to find out more information. They see a potential calamity and respond the only way they can, looking to reduce their exposure, accessing overseas derivative markets if they can.

In the alternative scenario, the PM and Analyst have the cell phone number of their investor relations contact and are about to call for an update. However, the IRO calls them first. While the IR Officer may be unable to discuss the cause of the incident, he can do two things:

1) Explain the importance of that plant to worldwide production, revenues and EBIT to the company as a whole, and
2) Reassure the investor that the company's management are on top of the situation, and are meeting to figure out next steps.

Does that mean the investor will not sell? Not necessarily. But as mentioned earlier, better that an investor sells on fundamentals rather than ignorance.

That is an example of proactive behavior by an investor relations team that at the very least builds credibility and respect, two factors that count for a lot in today's hyper-competitive investment world.

CHAPTER SEVEN

AFTERWORD

As methods of paying for company research from the brokerage community come under increasing scrutiny from regulatory agencies, asset managers will be encouraged to increase their own internal analytical resources. As a consequence, investor relations teams will find themselves dealing more often with experienced buy-side analysts whose demands will be just as great but whose attention span will be shorter.

Not because they have no interest in company fundamentals, quite the opposite. They will only need to cover a smaller percentage of their universe, in pursuit of specific investments that suit their style and which they can analyze in depth and truly understand. (This is different to sell-side research that looks to cover large segments of individual sectors, allowing the analyst to create relative research that becomes a credible body of knowledge.)

Investor relations teams will need to be responsive to these shifting demands, by focusing their message, keeping current with the concerns of the marketplace and nurturing relationships with core investors. In other words, recognizing the increasingly competitive nature of the investment markets and resolving to win.

This book will not provide the complete answer to each company's specific issues – every company is different in both its operations and the impact of external economic and market forces – but offers you a broad series of guideposts on how to excel at communications.

The topics covered in this book included:

Expectations, management and fulfillment;
Communication skills;
Preparation for meetings;
Knowing your audience;
Confronting harsh realities;
Proactive behaviors;
Common problems and mistakes.

In using the recommendations and advice offered in this book, investor relations professionals can adopt a simple approach that will serve them well in their communications with investors.

Remember these three behaviors:

Tell the facts about your company's performance
Explain how the company achieved that performance
Share what the company is going to do next.

Finally, to help you achieve the perfect meeting, I have created a repeatable checklist that can be used to monitor your progress as you prepare for any contact with the outside world. The list can be downloaded from my website;

valorinvestmentsllc.com

This list lays out the various tasks that the investor relations team should complete in preparation for any meaningful contact with its constituents: shareholders; the media; employees; and the public.

As with all regularly performed activities, these pre- and post-meeting behaviors will become second nature to the well-organized IR operation.

But, of course, every company is different and you may wish to seek advice as to the best approach, depending on your size, industry, geography and needs. My contact details are on my website.

Jonathan L. Passmore
Principal
Valor IR Consulting
Fairfield, CT, USA

Other topics to explore but excluded from this guide book:

Shareholder Outreach & Engagement:
Searching for, and keeping core investors

The Rise in Corporate Governance Standards:
How changing Boards can drive the process

Personnel Training:
Coaching for IR professionals, Executives and Board Members

Investor Styles:
The needs, wants and must-haves of institutional investors

The author, Jonathan L. Passmore has worked in the investment industry since 1975, in fixed income and public equity, as an institutional broker, and, from 2001 to 2014, as a senior portfolio manager of international equity at one of America's largest corporate pension funds.

Jonathan's experiences, based both in London and New York combine a deep knowledge of investment markets, vehicles, styles and strategies with focused, professional communication skills developed over the last four decades. In addition, his analytical skills help him articulate the complexities of our world in a clear, concise, unambiguous form, making him uniquely qualified to advise publicly-listed companies on their approach to institutional investors in the English-speaking world.

www.ingramcontent.com/pod-product-compliance
Lightning Source LLC
Chambersburg PA
CBHW071125210326
41519CB00020B/6429